DEDICATION

*To physics, to chemistry, and to the laws of nature,
for collectively they somehow produce everything
in the observable universe.*

*To the electromagnetic spectrum (and thus to photons),
for providing us with all that we see around us.*

Without them, none of this would have been possible.

They are truly the unsung heroes of immortal time.

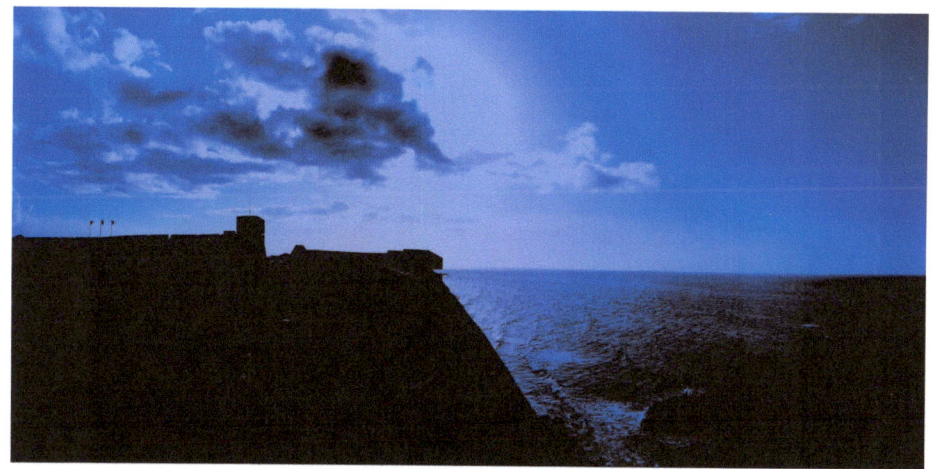

FOREWORD

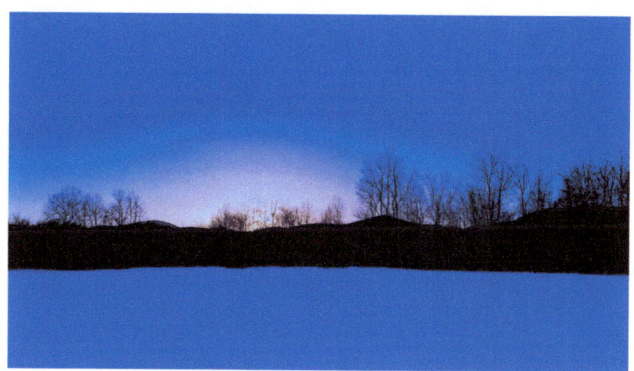

Ever since I can remember, blue has always been my favorite color, in any of its hues, tints, or shades.

I strongly suspect that it is for that same reason that the ocean and the sky fascinate me, for you should know that I am drawn to them as life is drawn to water.

And so in my brief and sporadic Earthly travels, I keep my eyes wide open for the blue around me, which I desperately try to capture with my camera. The task is utopian for I believe I will never be able to achieve the impossible... nothing can replicate the depth and the intensity and the surrealness of these blue hues when painted by the hand of the cosmos, observed in the living, breathing moment.

I also enjoy altering the photographs as I see fit, in an effort to convey—even if it is in the tiniest of forms—its magnificence.

Peace, cheers, and may these images inspire you to keep your eyes open for the blue that is all around you.

Quantum Line Wave

July 2015

Las Vegas, Nevada

Quantum Wave Line

July 2015

Las Vegas, Nevada

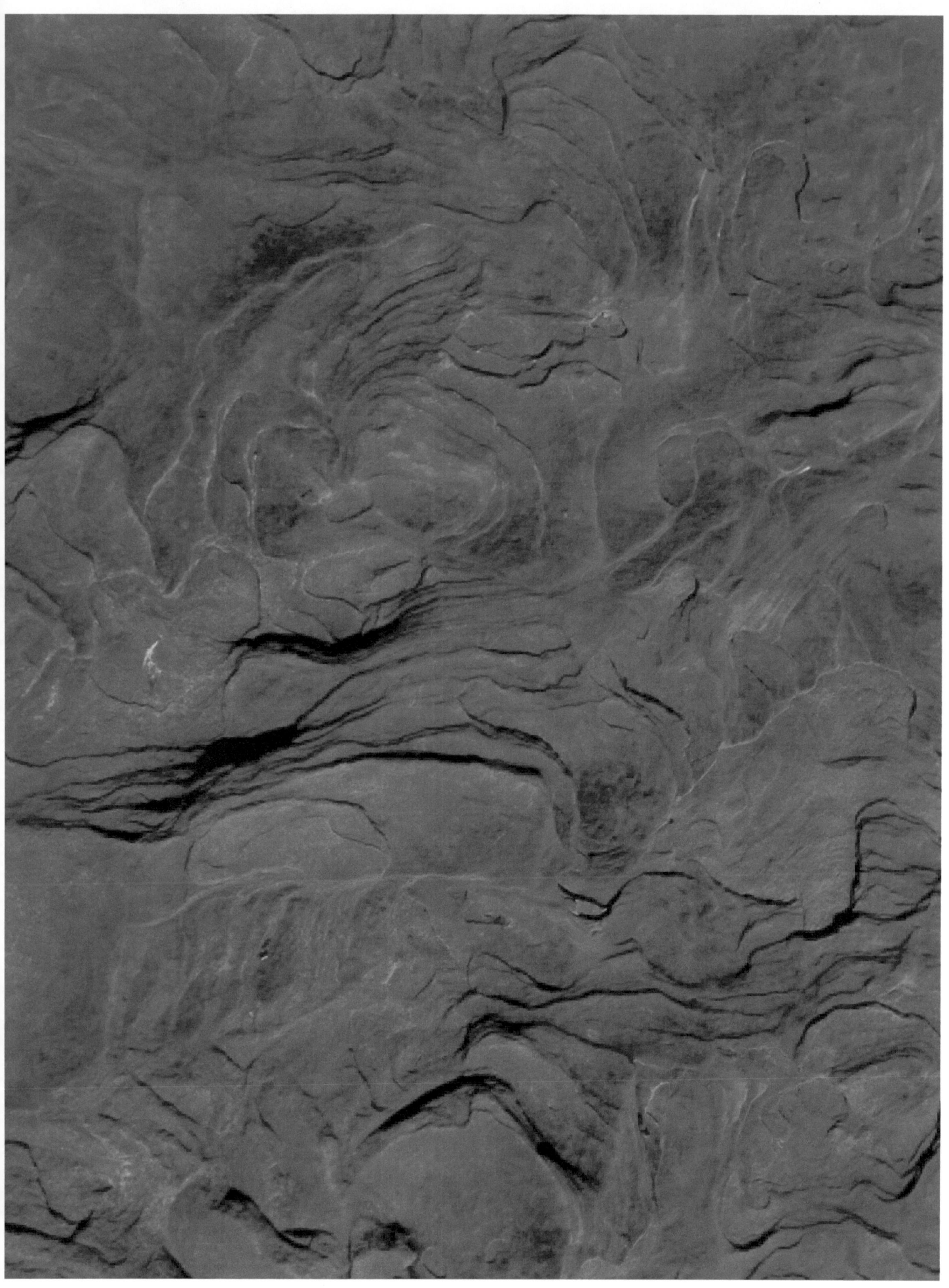

Blue Rock Canyon

July 2015

Grand Canyon, Arizona

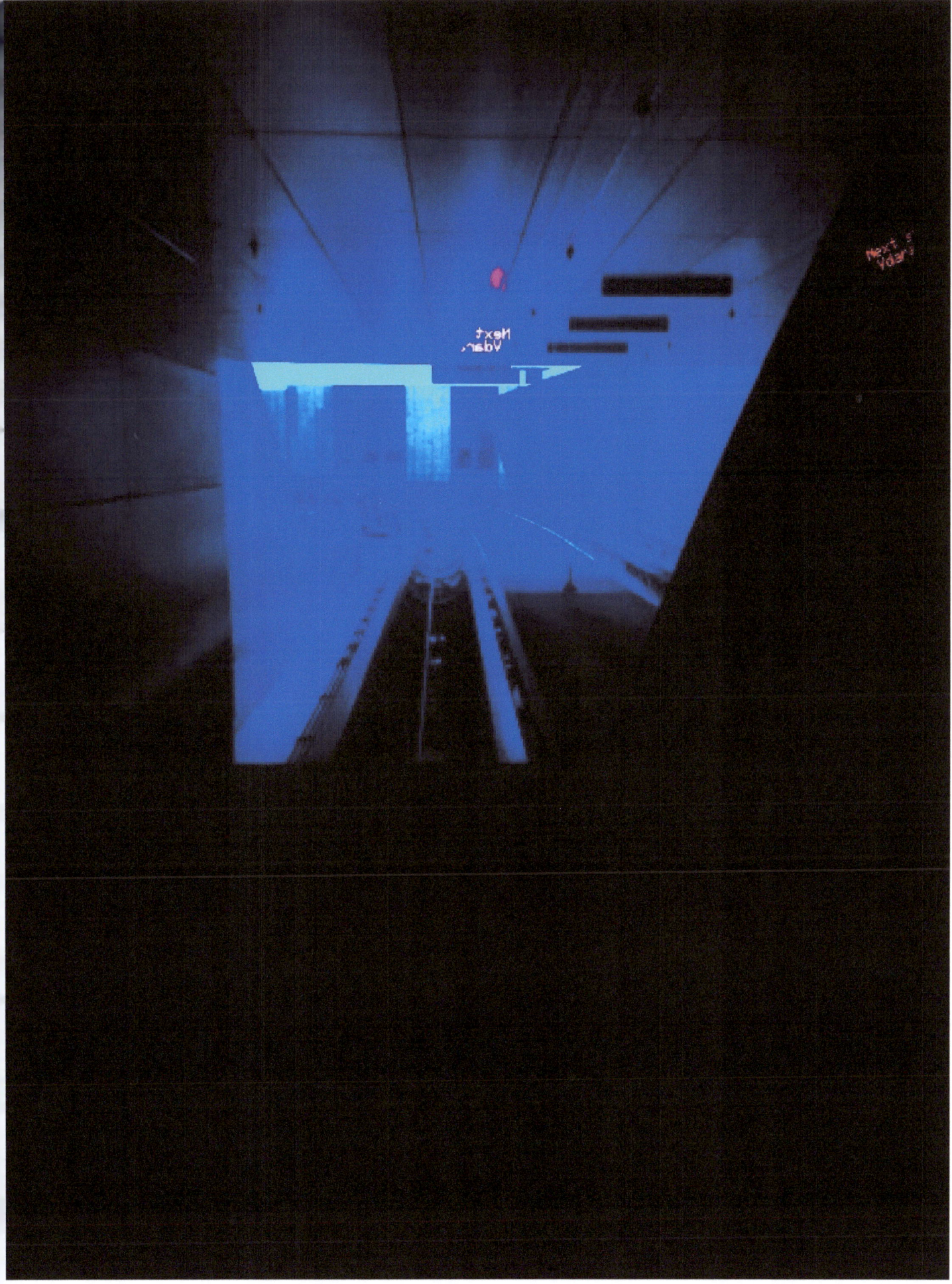

Into the Blue

July 2015

Las Vegas, Nevada

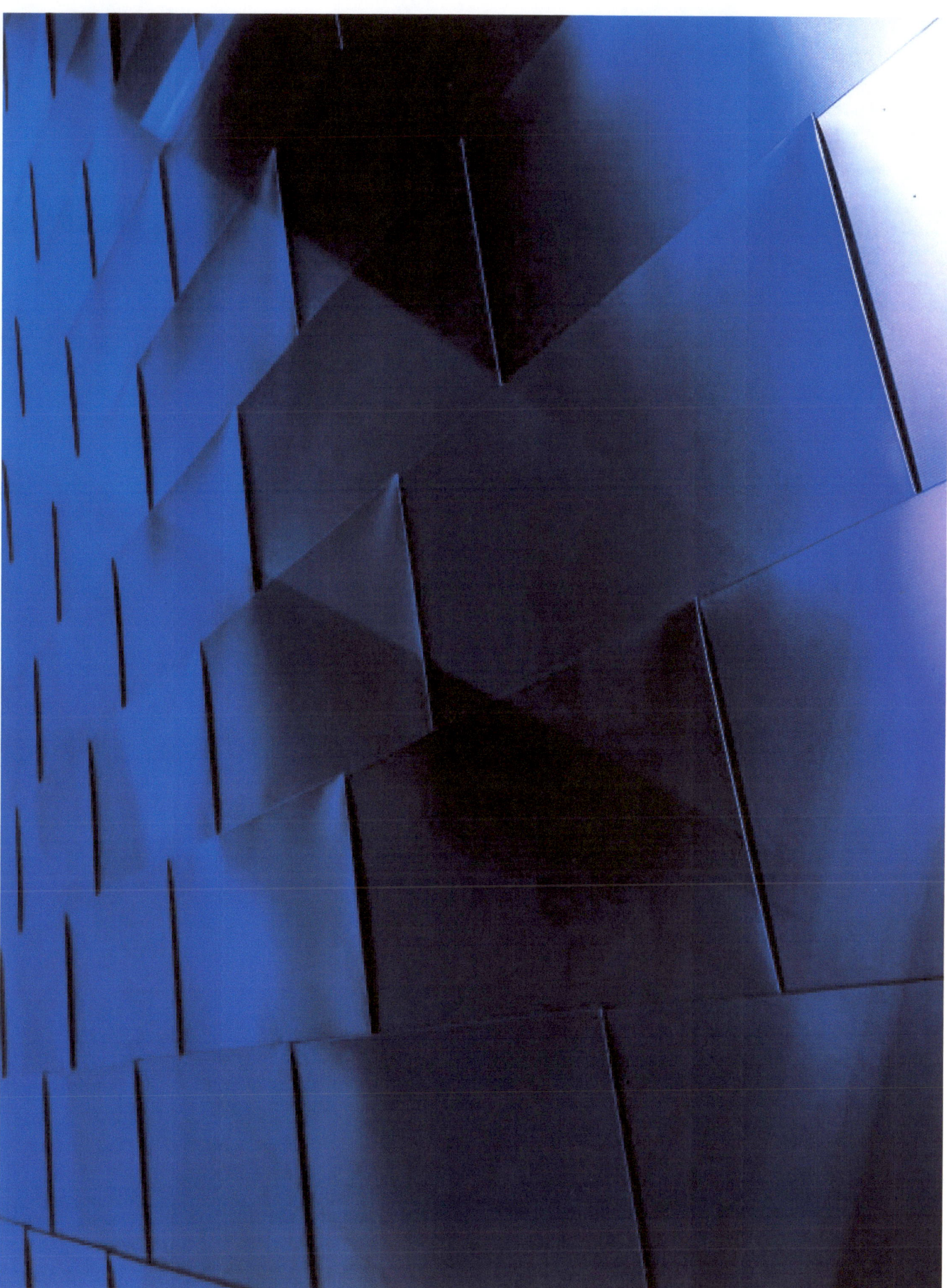

The Blue Wall

July 2015

Las Vegas, Nevada

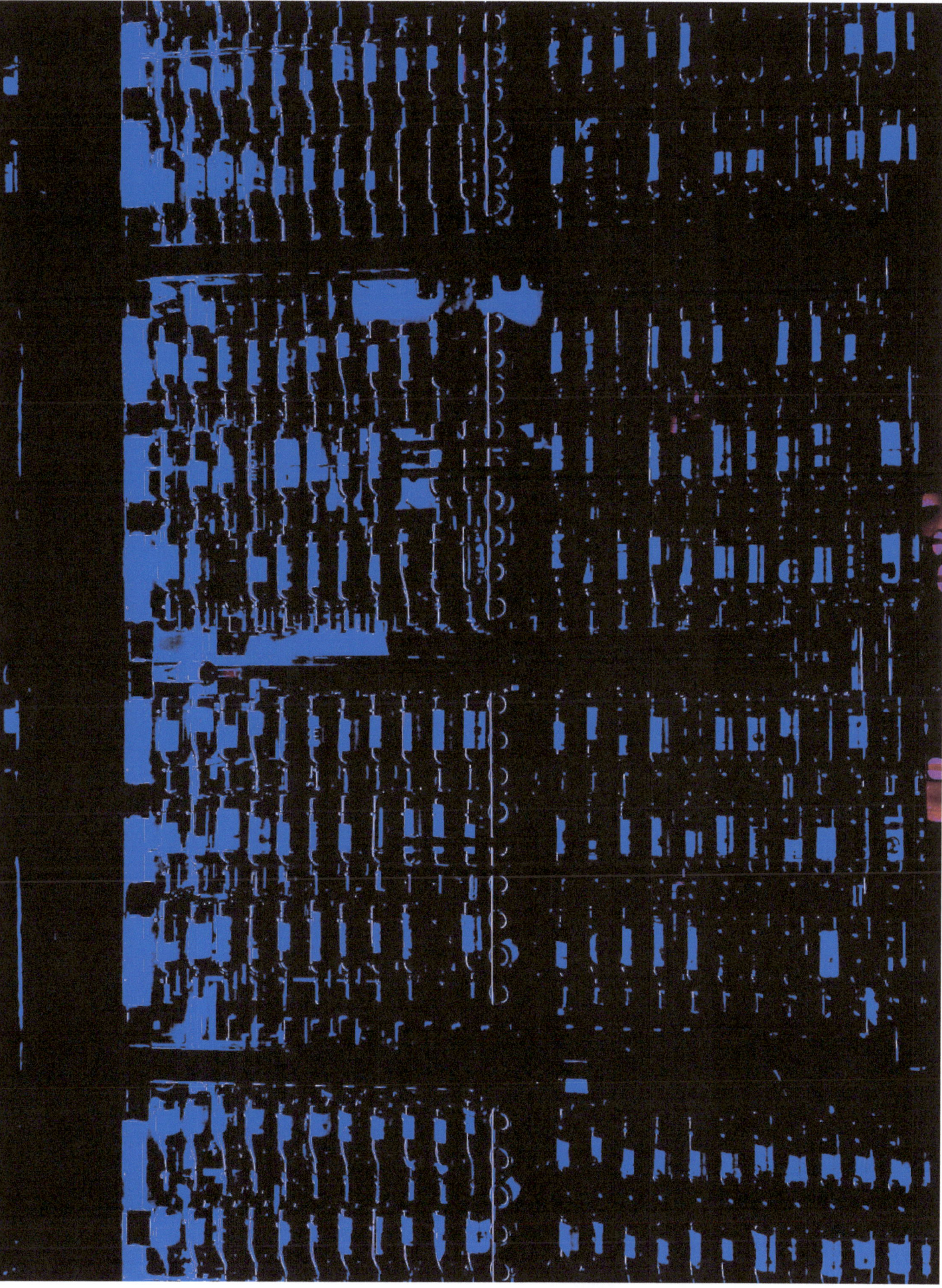

Blue Cellar

September 2012

Delray Beach, Florida

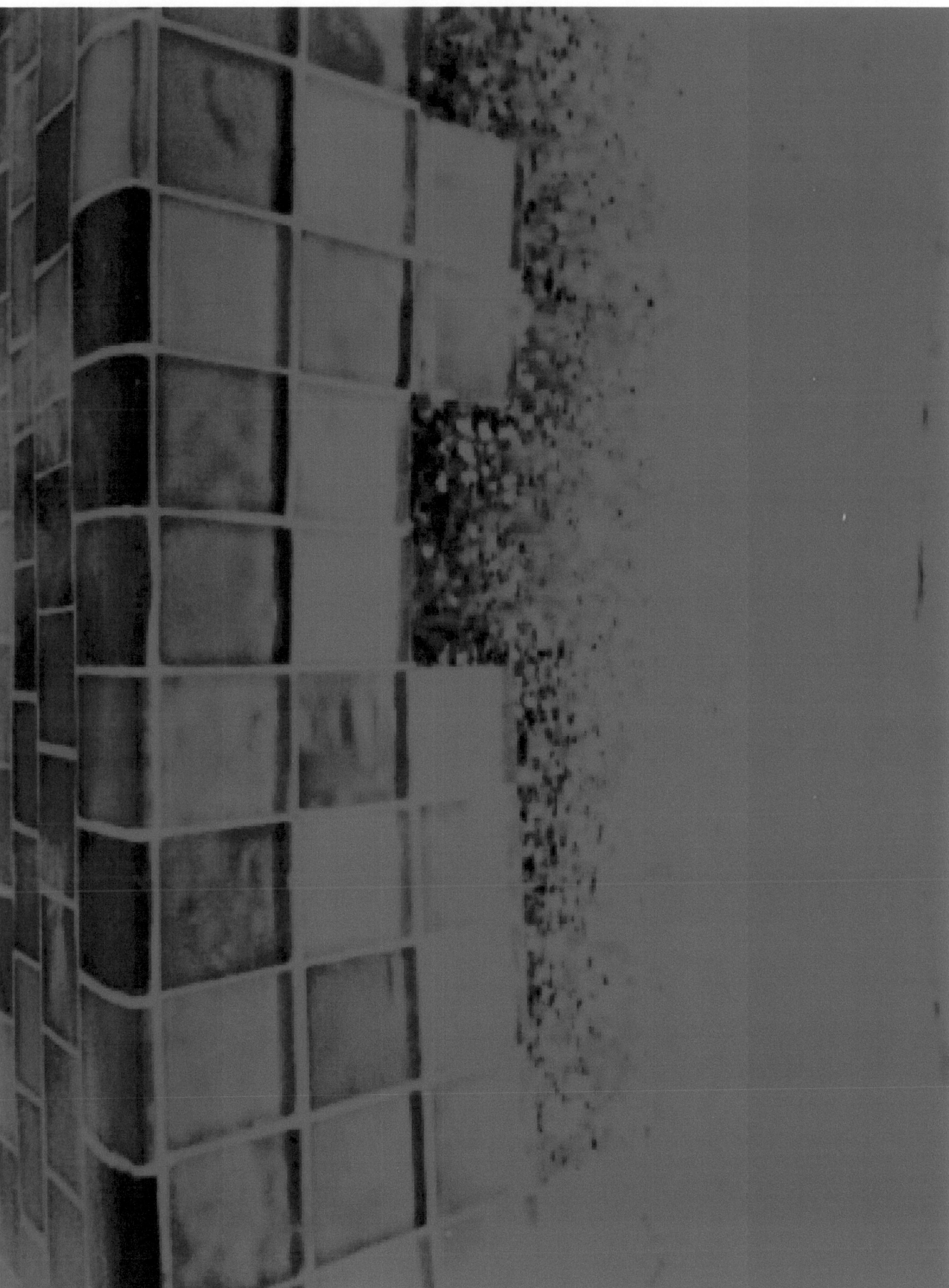

Electric Blue

January 2015

West Palm Beach, Florida

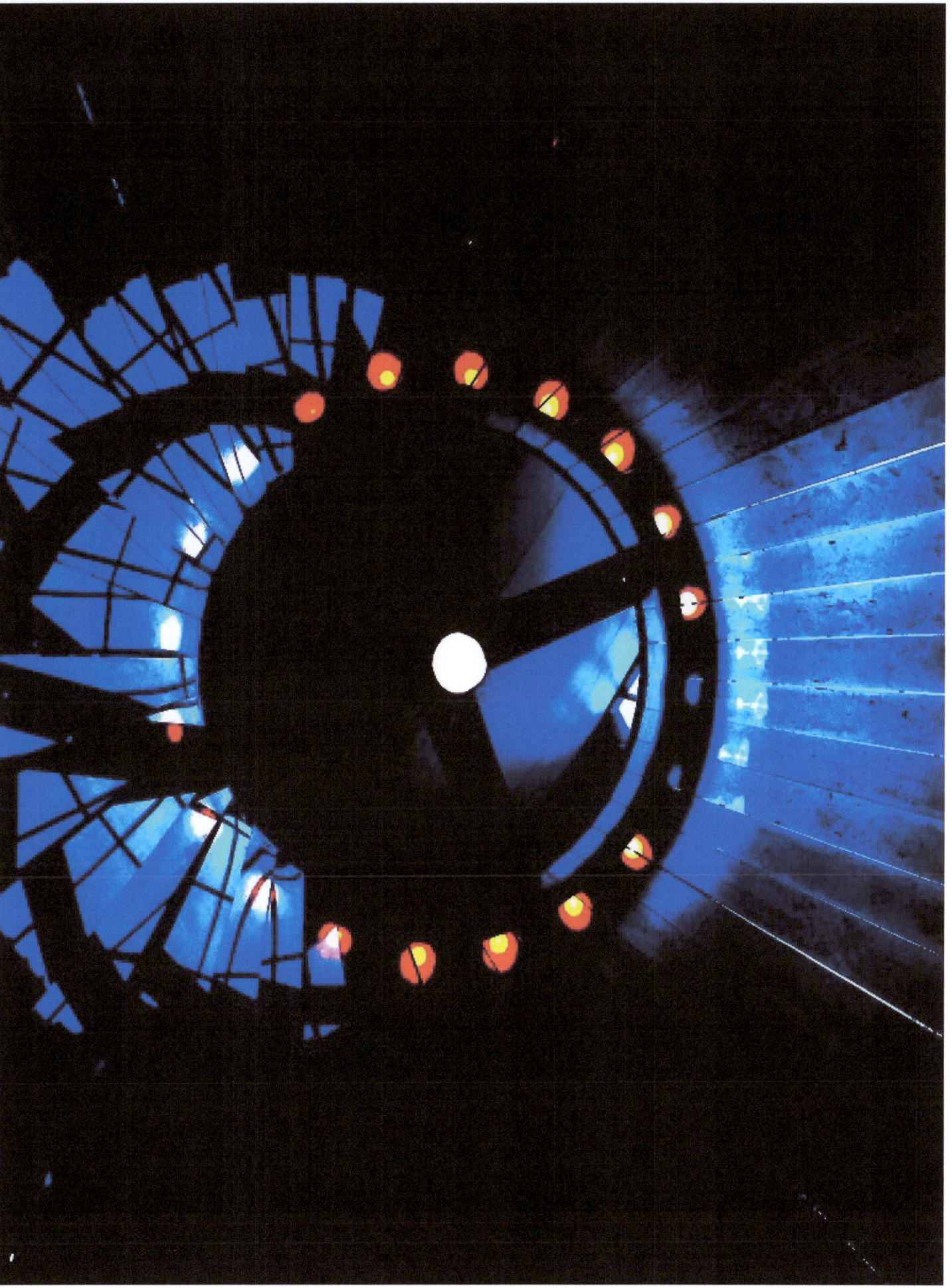

Blue Kaleidoscope

July 2013

Los Angeles, California

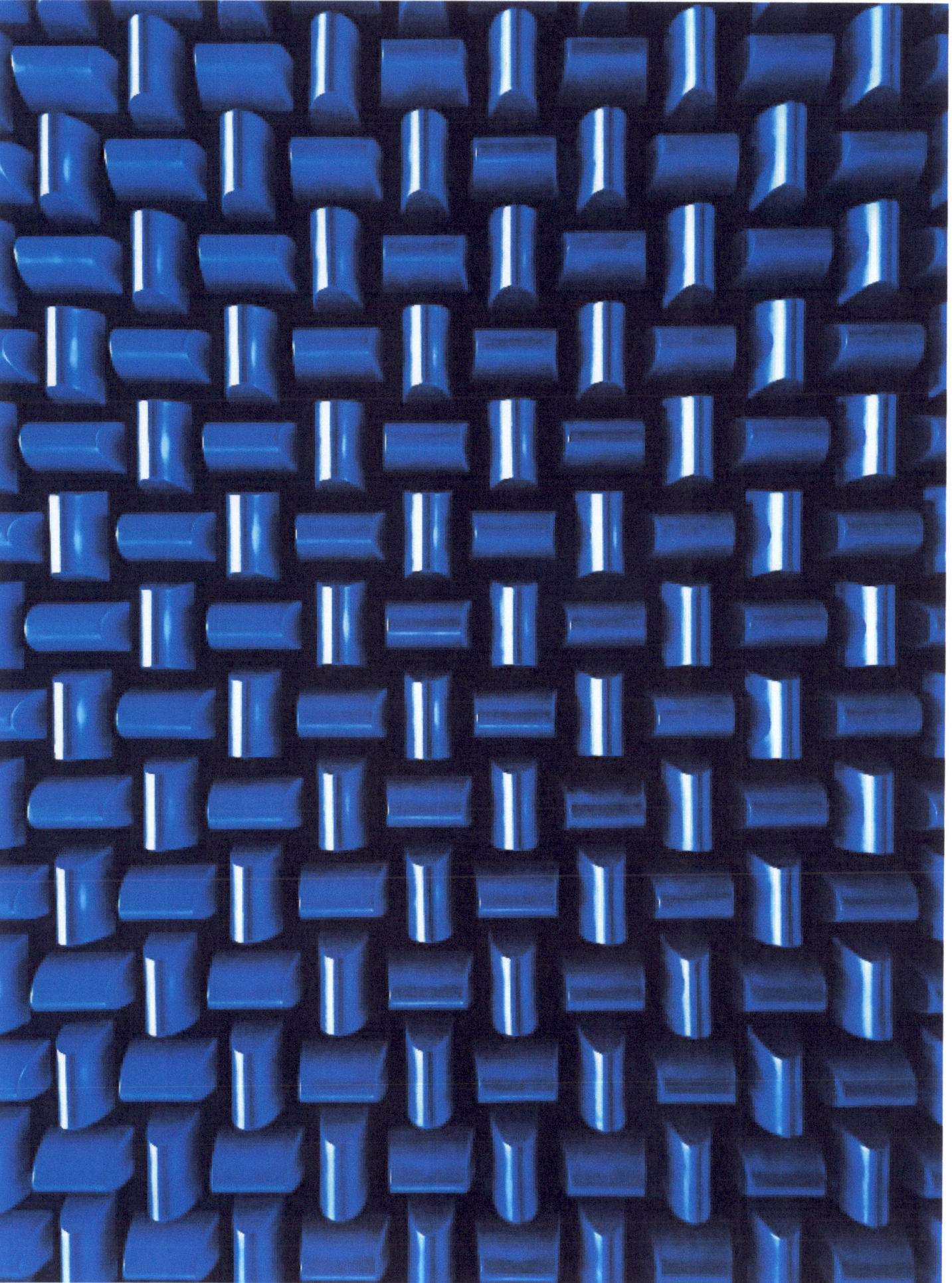

The Blue Wall II

July 2015

Las Vegas, Nevada

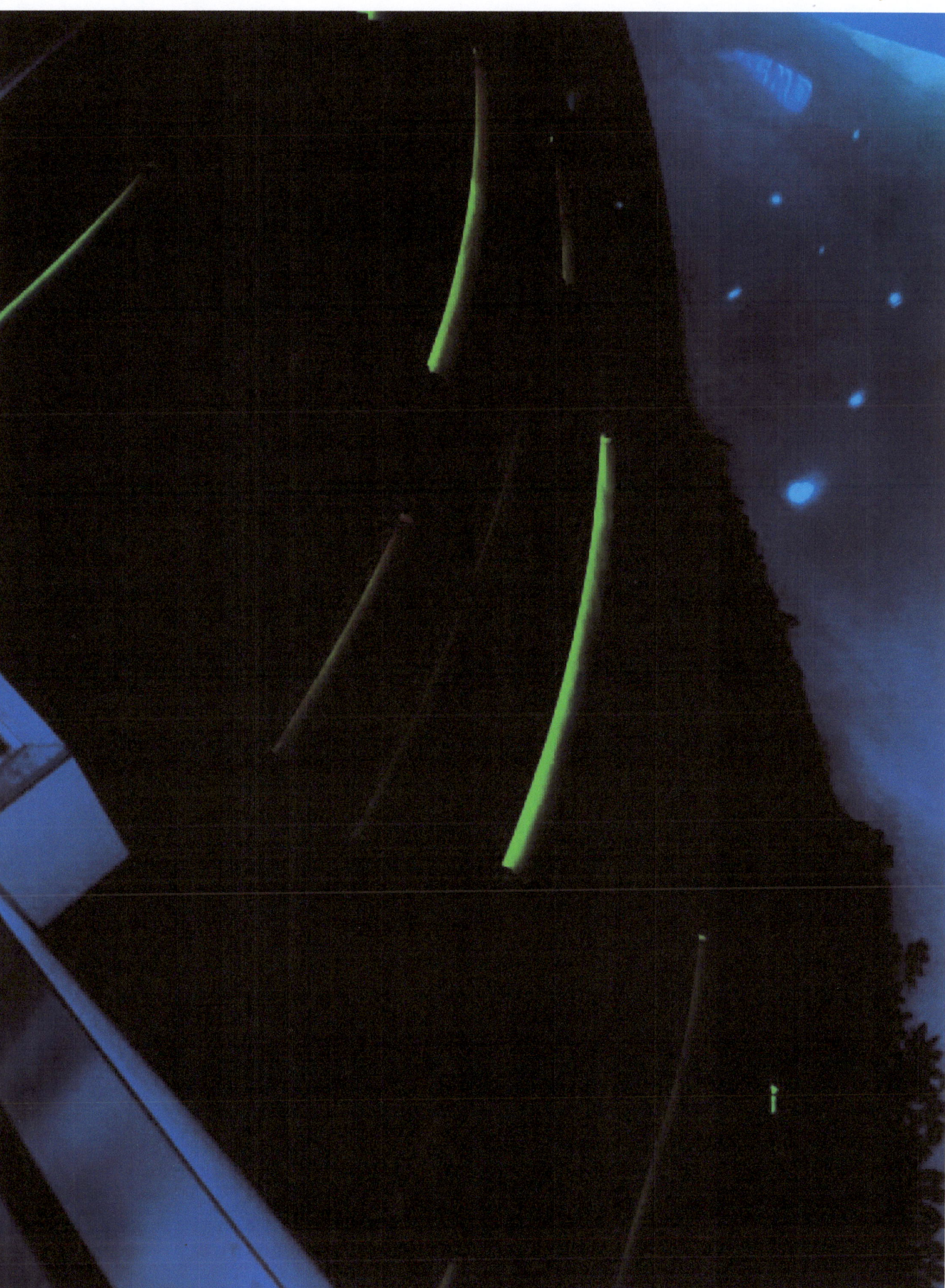

Cosmic Blue

July 2015

Las Vegas, Nevada

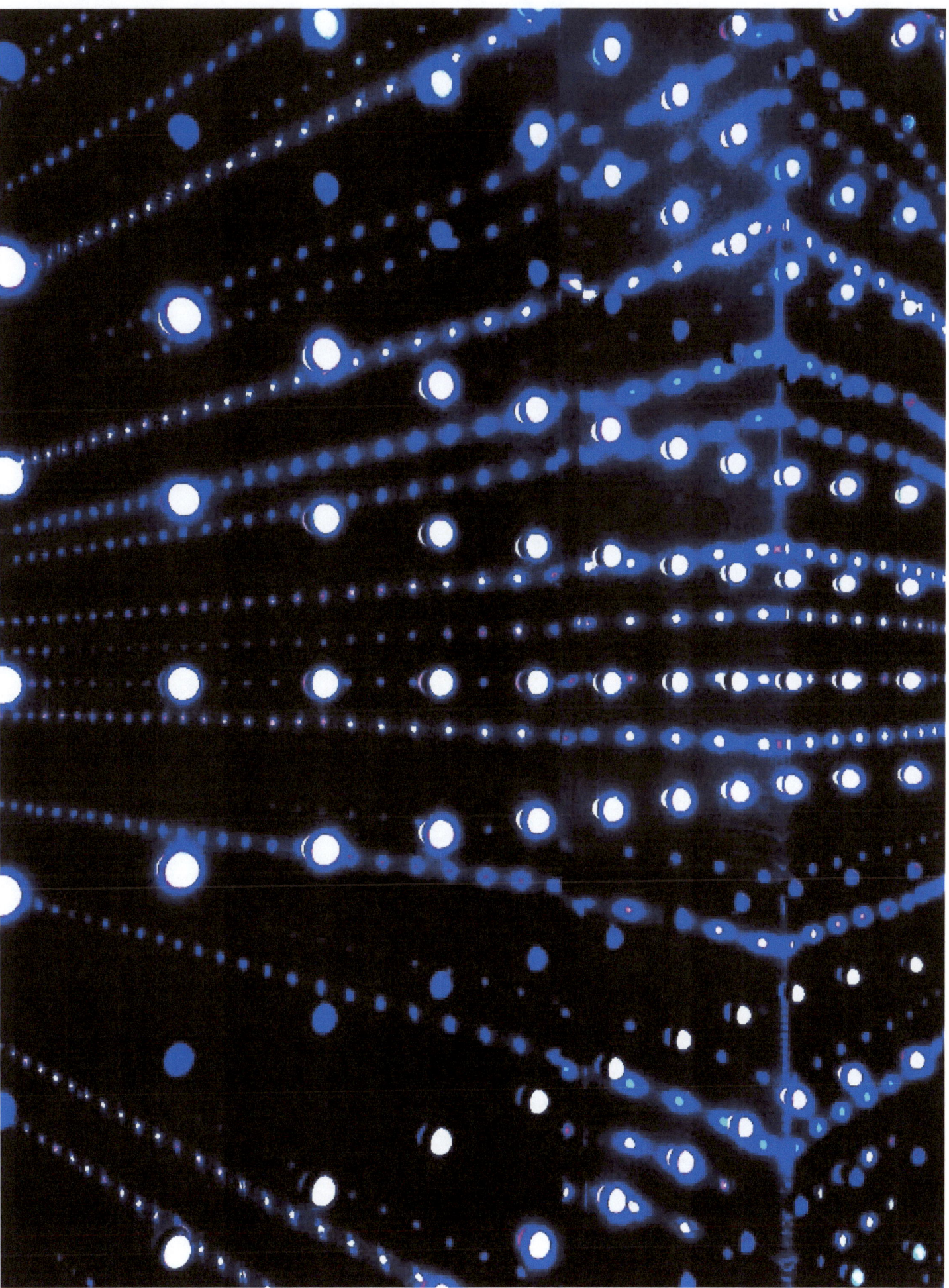

Blue Matrix

July 2015

Las Vegas, Nevada

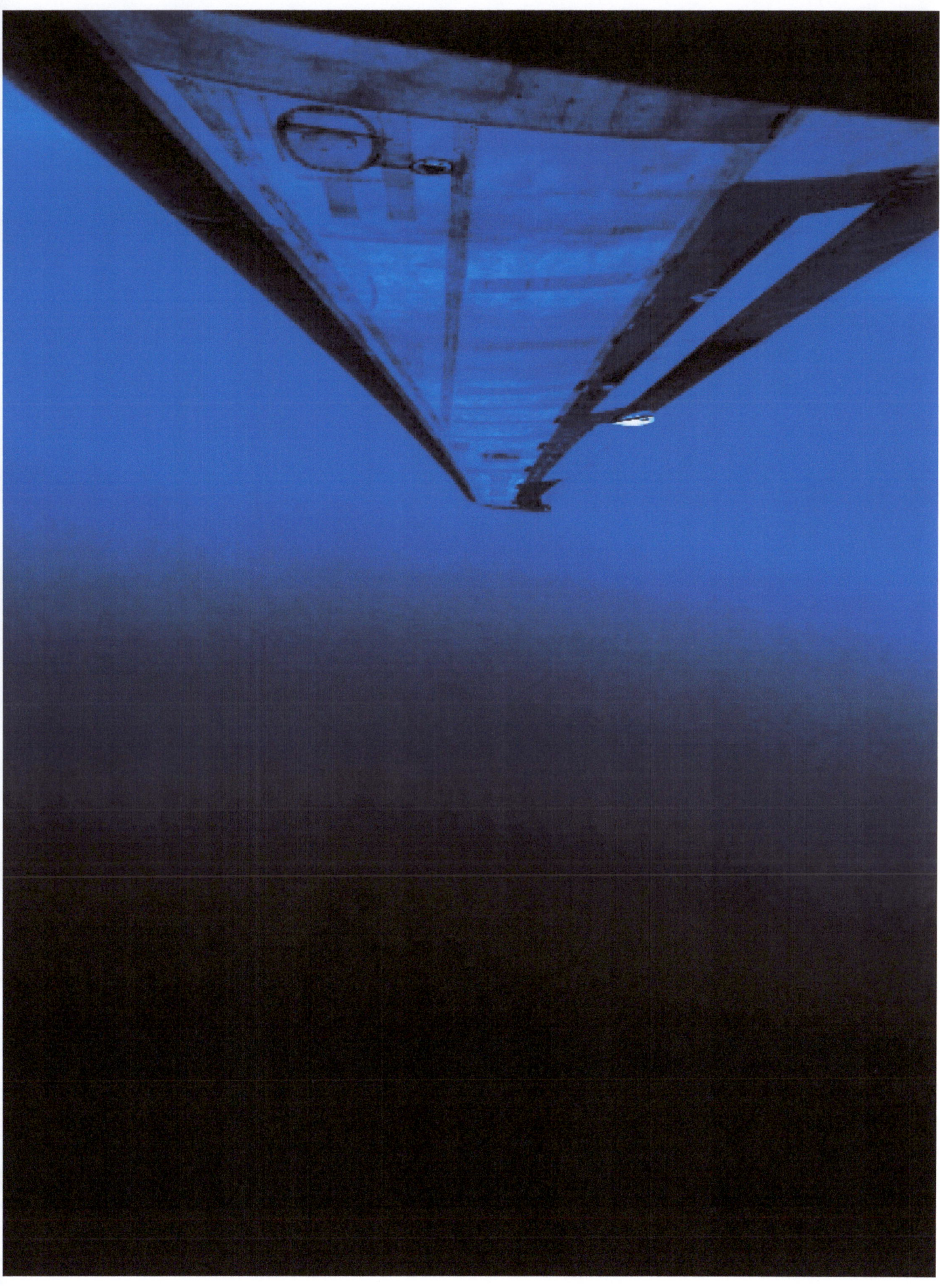

Blue Metal Wing

June 2010

International Air Space, Earth

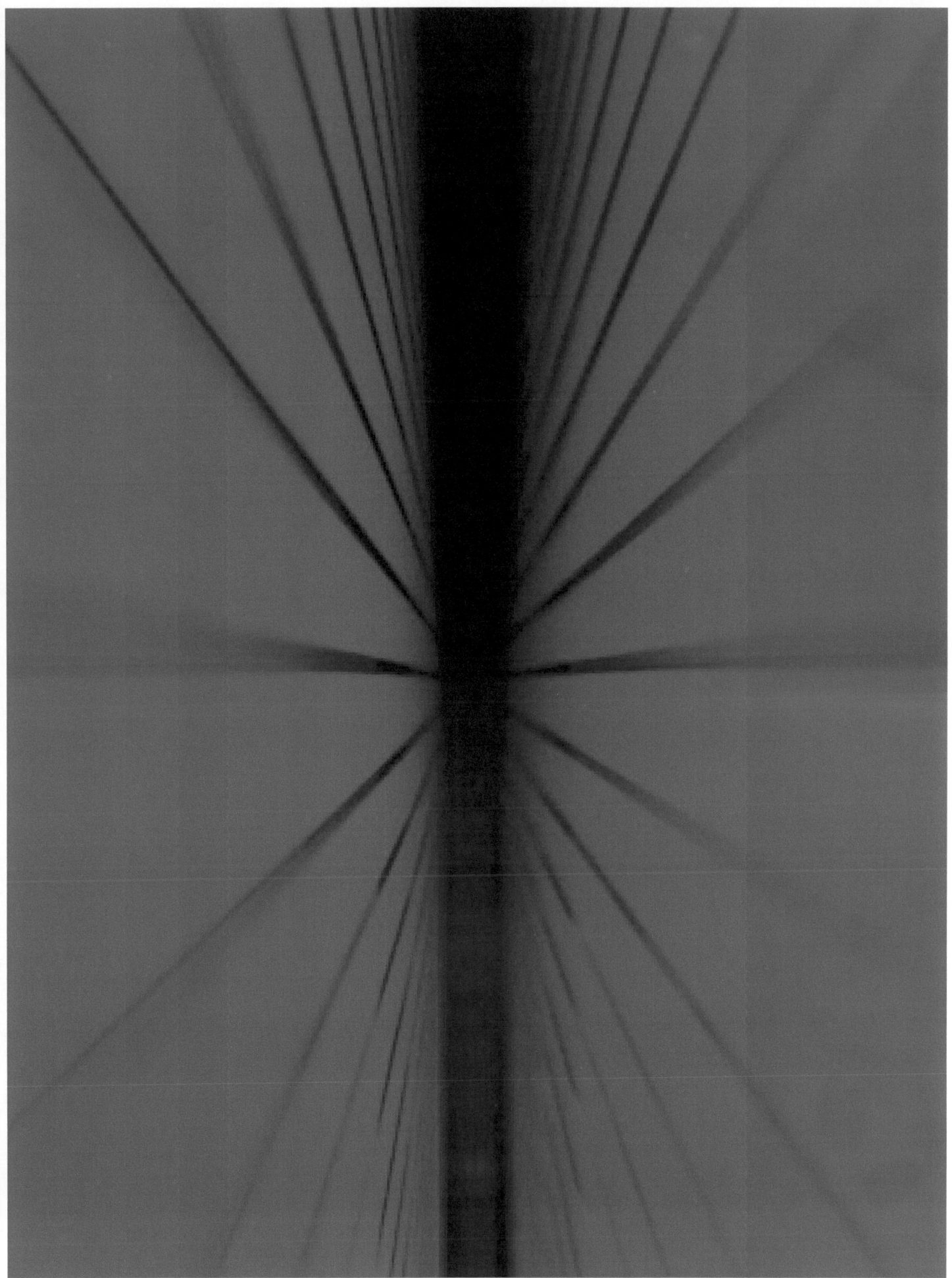

Blue Horizon

December 2014

New York, New York

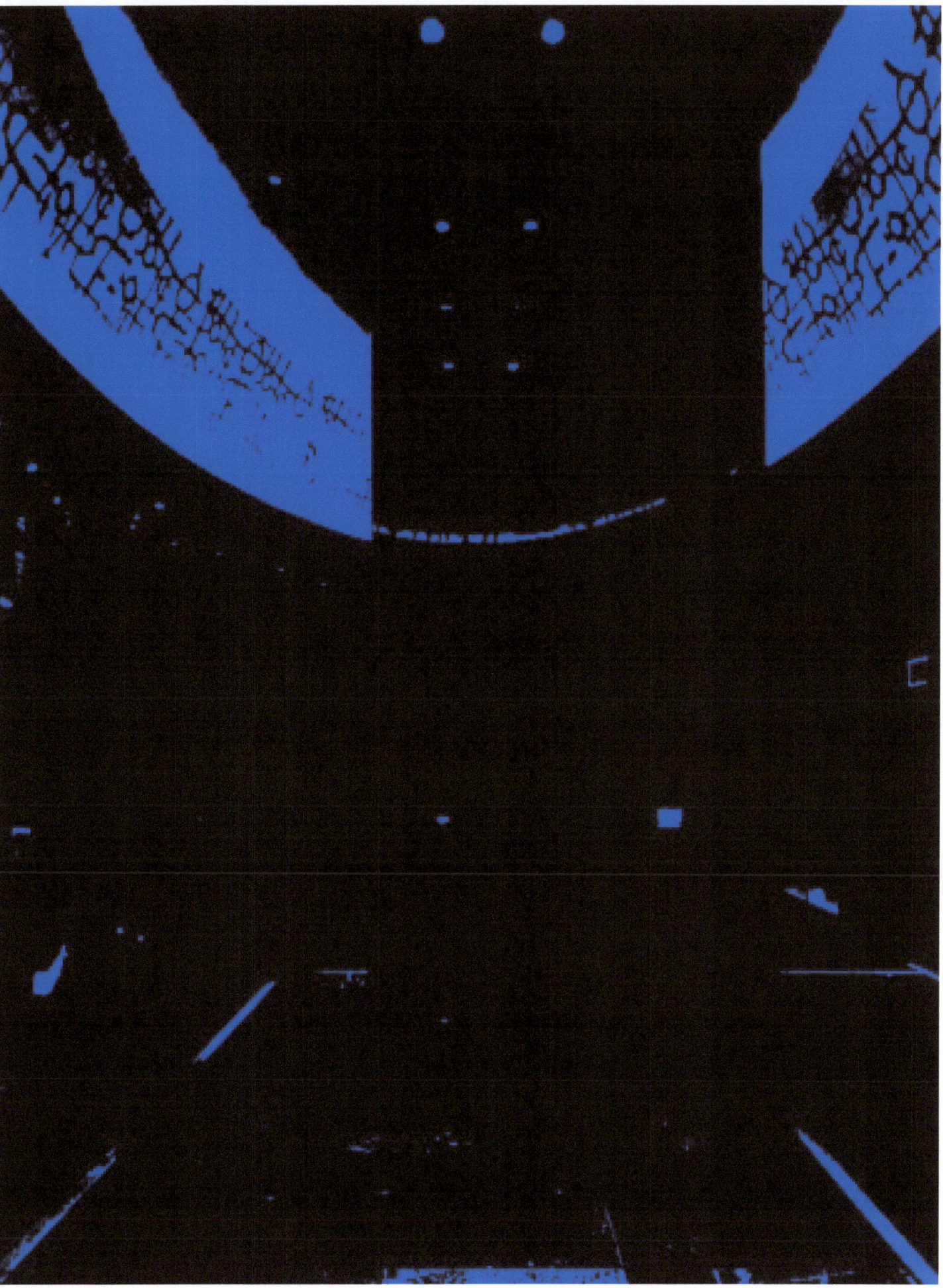

Abstract Blue

July 2015

Las Vegas, Nevada

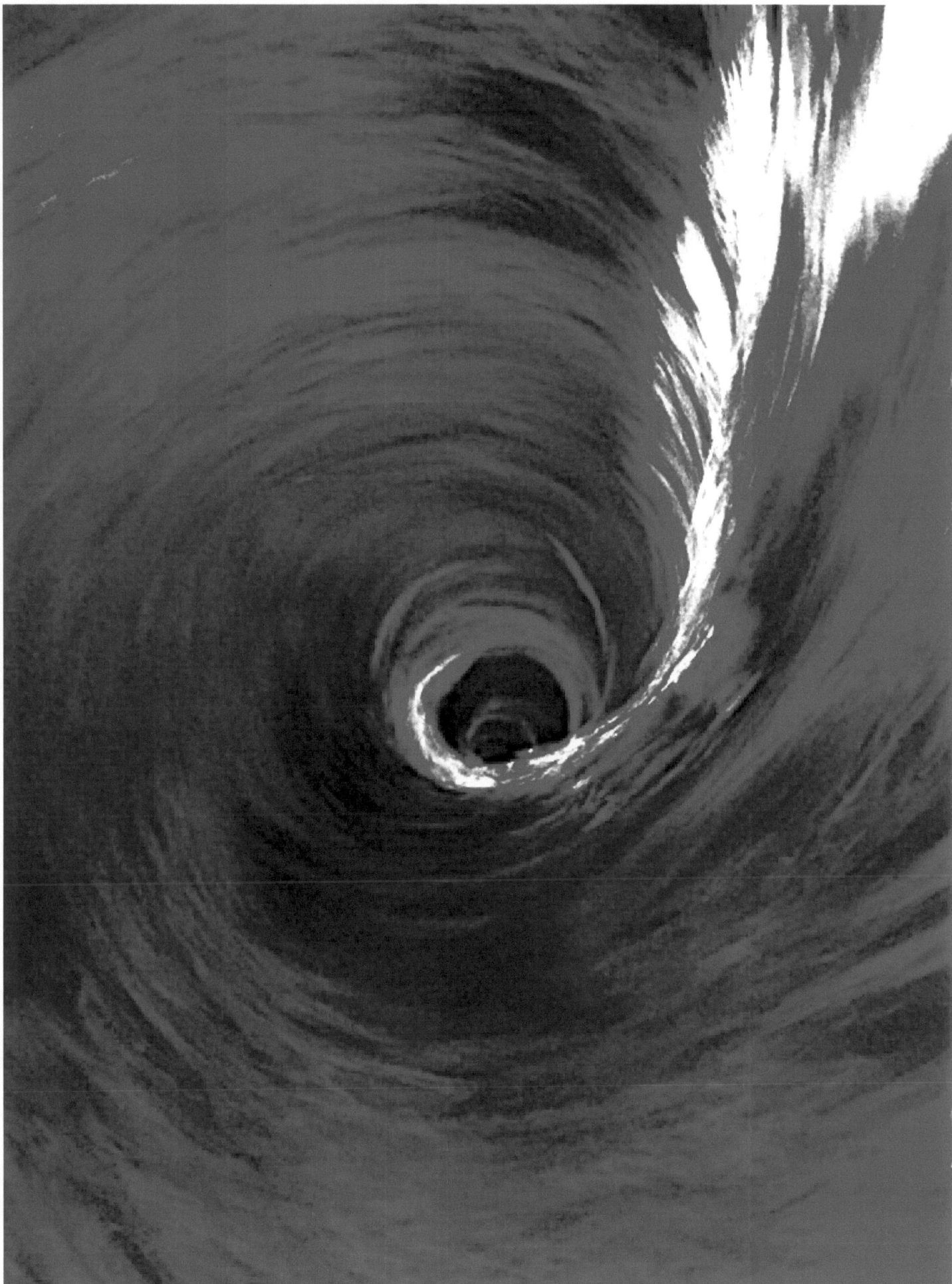

The Blue Vortex

July 2015

Las Vegas, Nevada

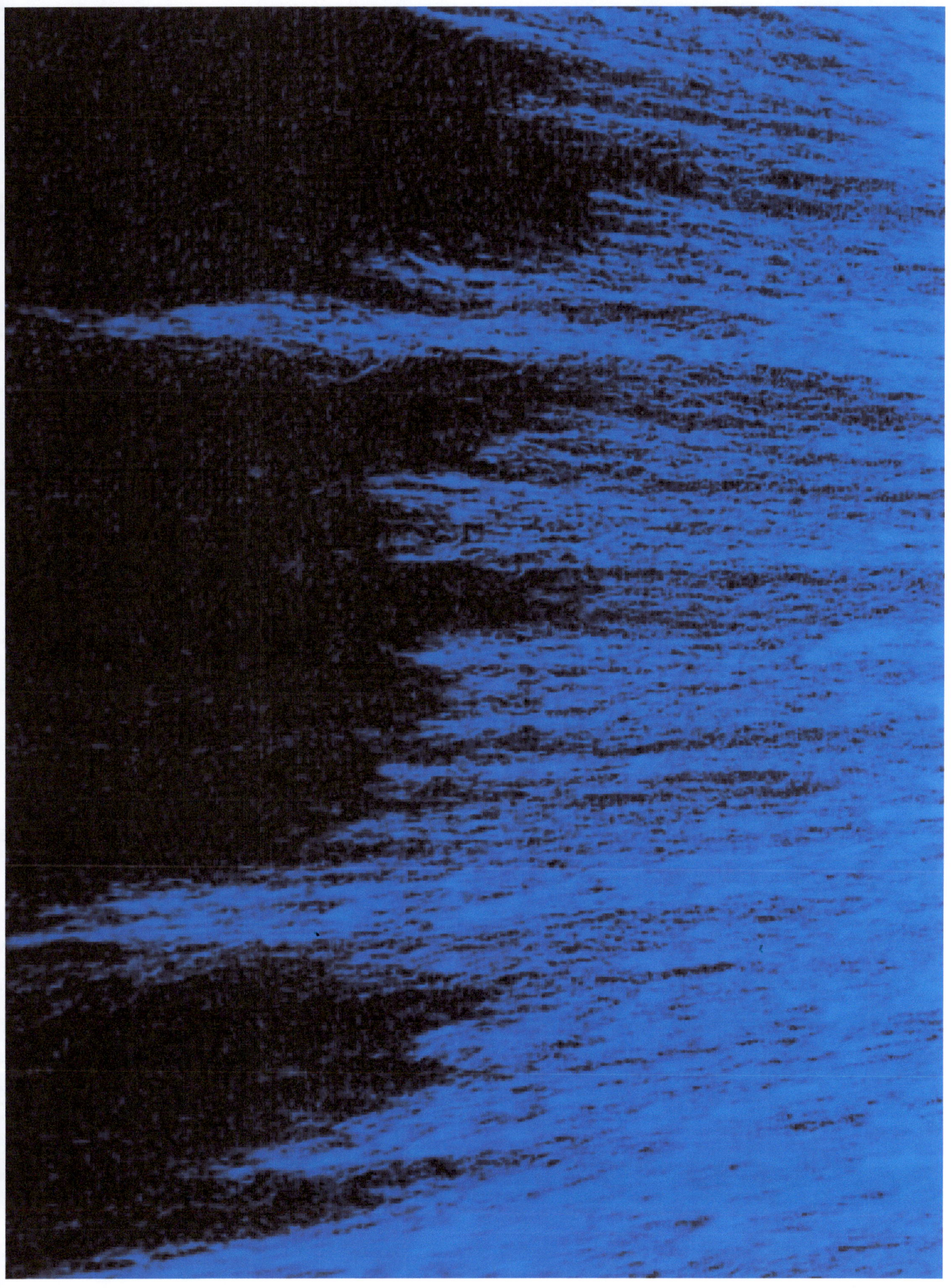

Blue Chaos

July 2015

Las Vegas, Nevada

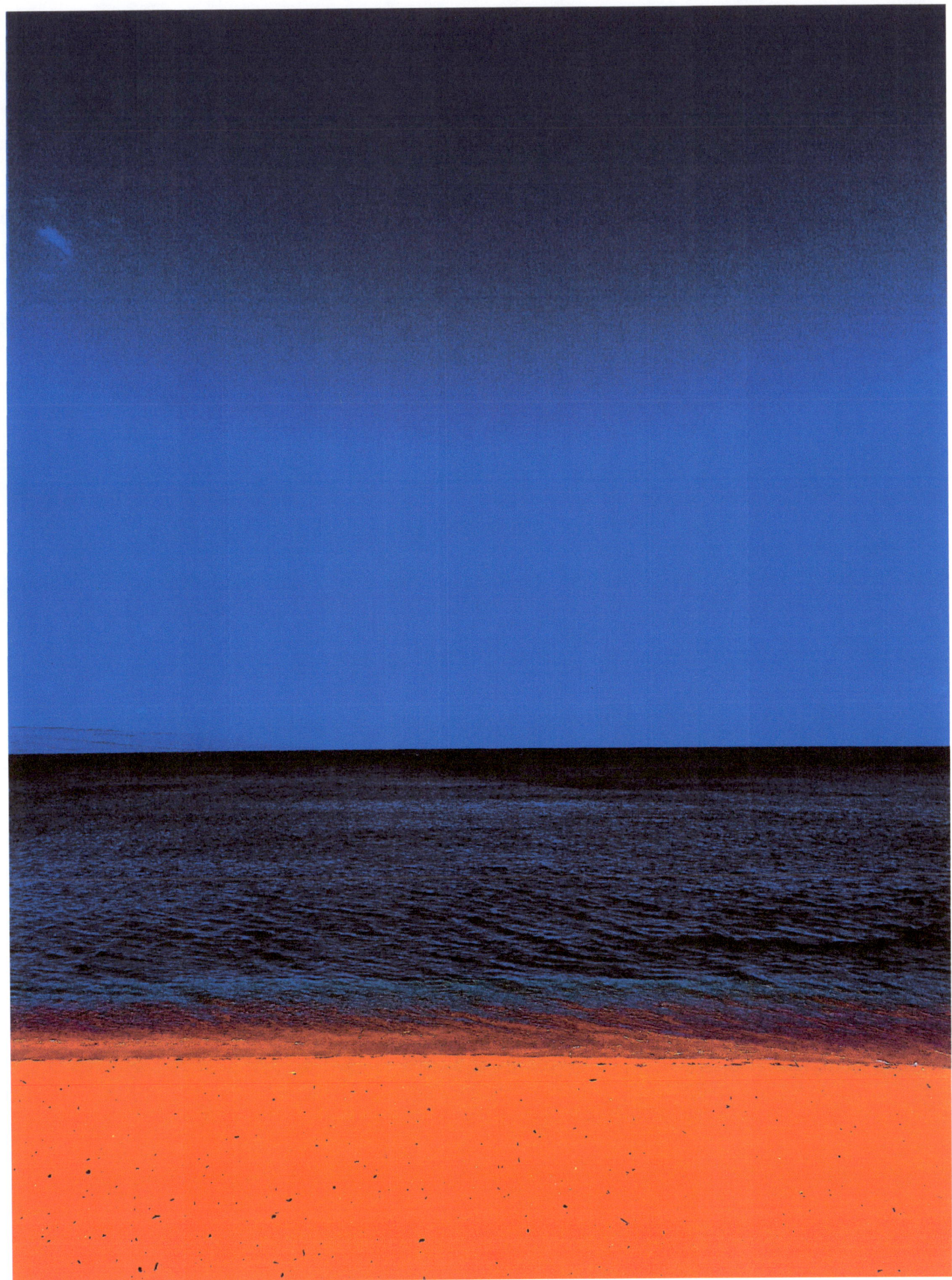

Blue Sky and Sea with Red Beach

July 2014

Maui, Hawaii

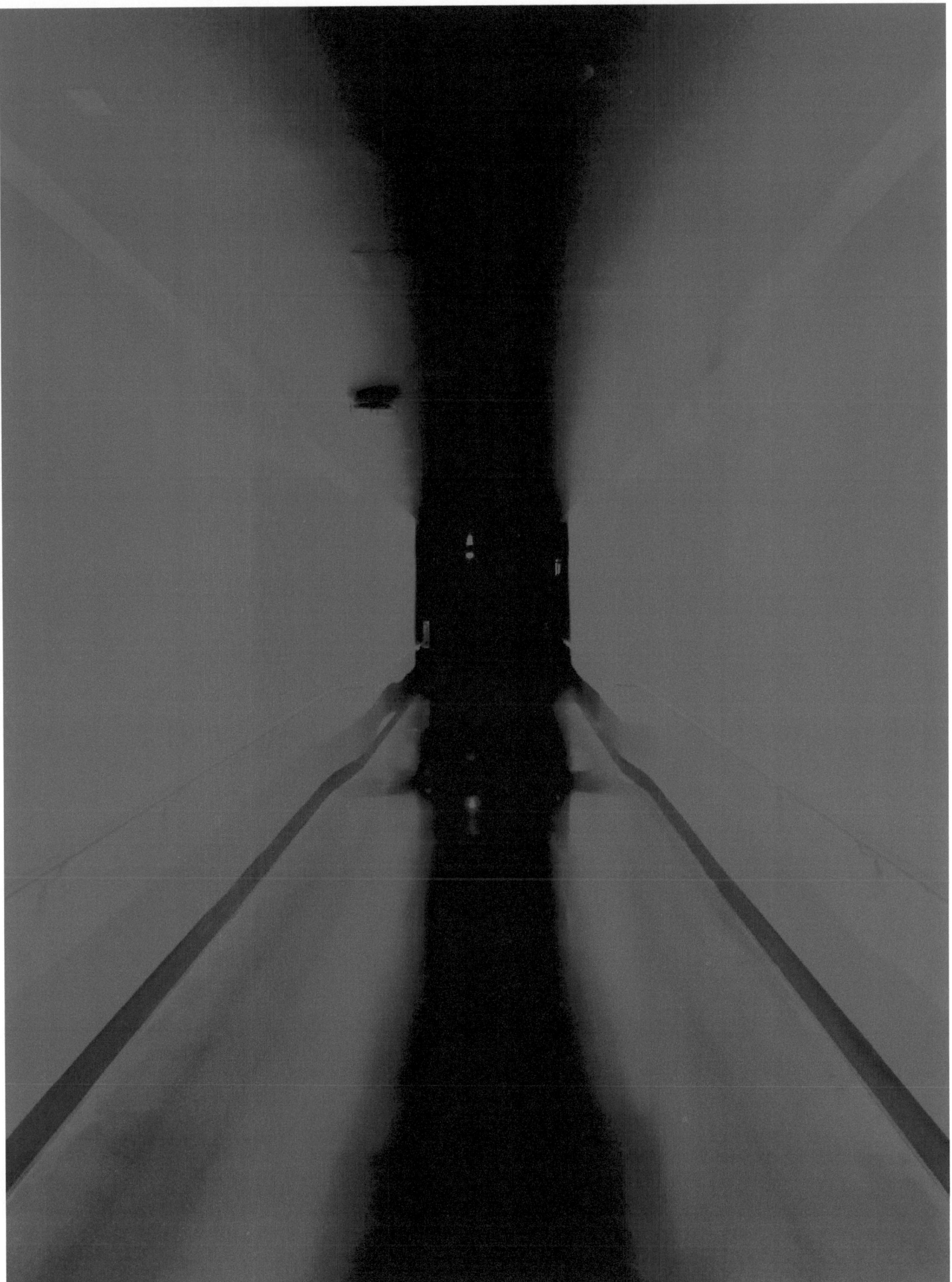

Blue Passageway

June 2014

Cape Canaveral, Florida

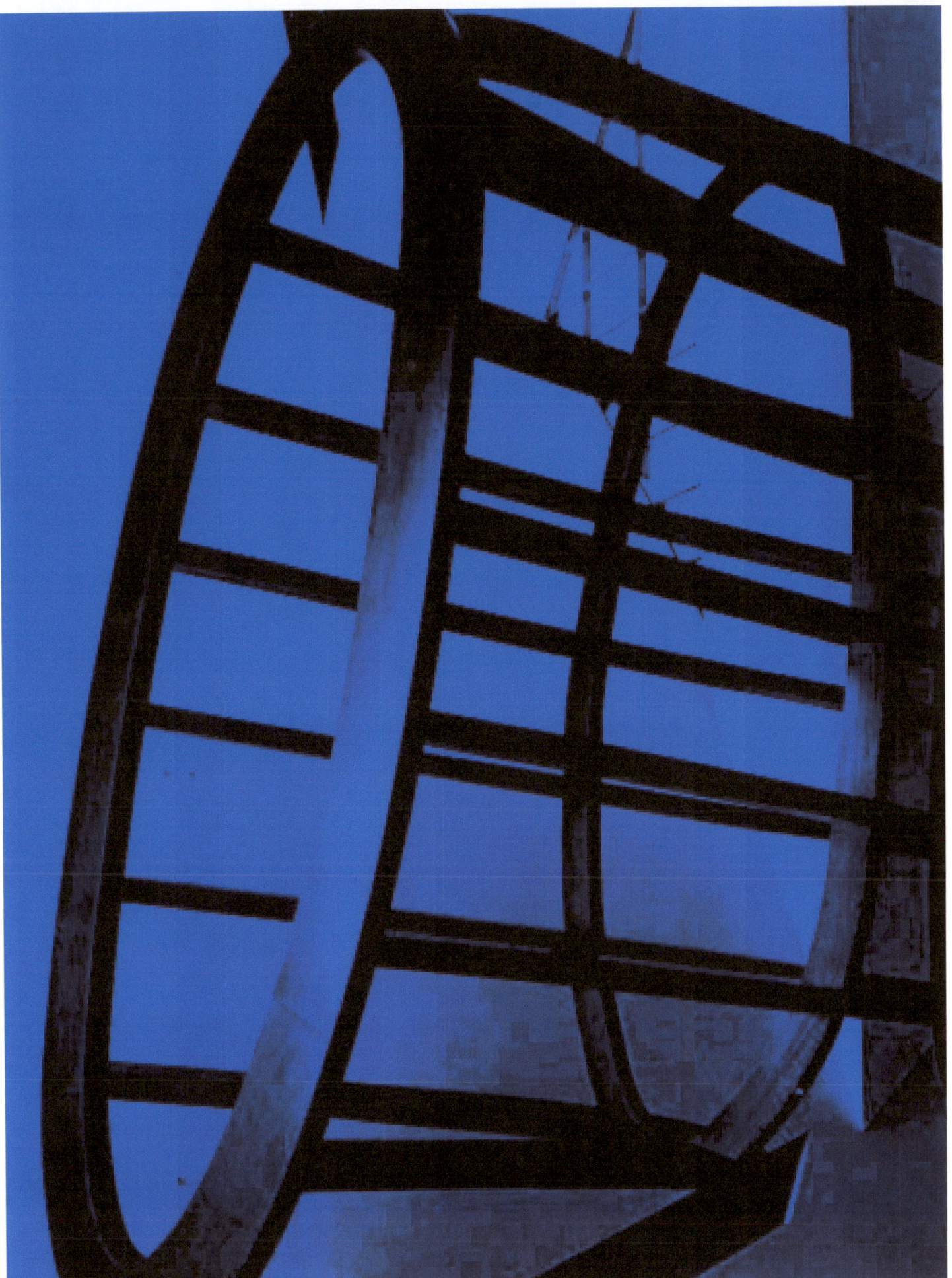

Circles in Blue

July 2015

Las Vegas, Nevada

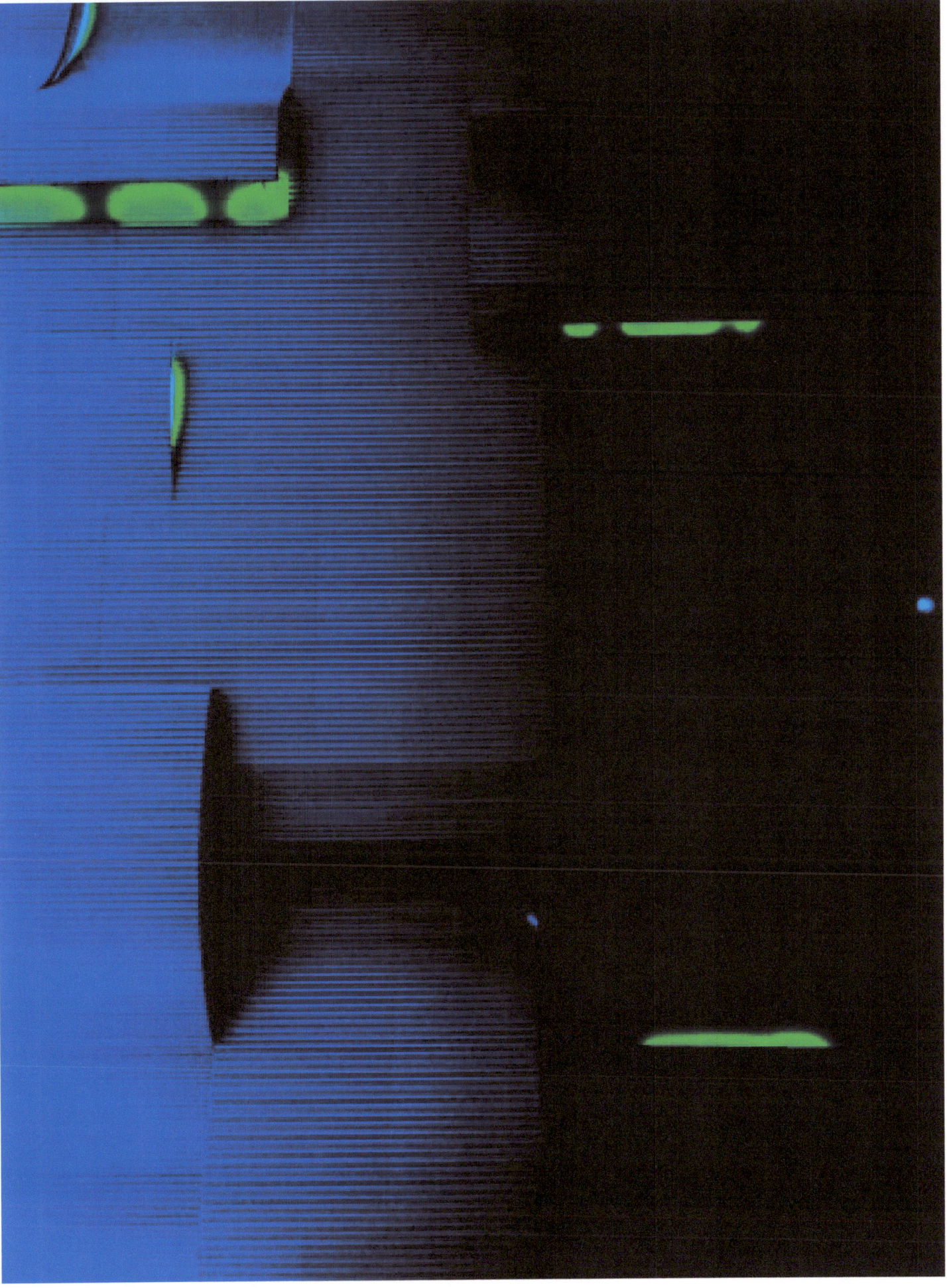

Blue Metal Facade

July 2015

Las Vegas, Nevada

Blue Night with Moon

June 2014

Orlando, Florida

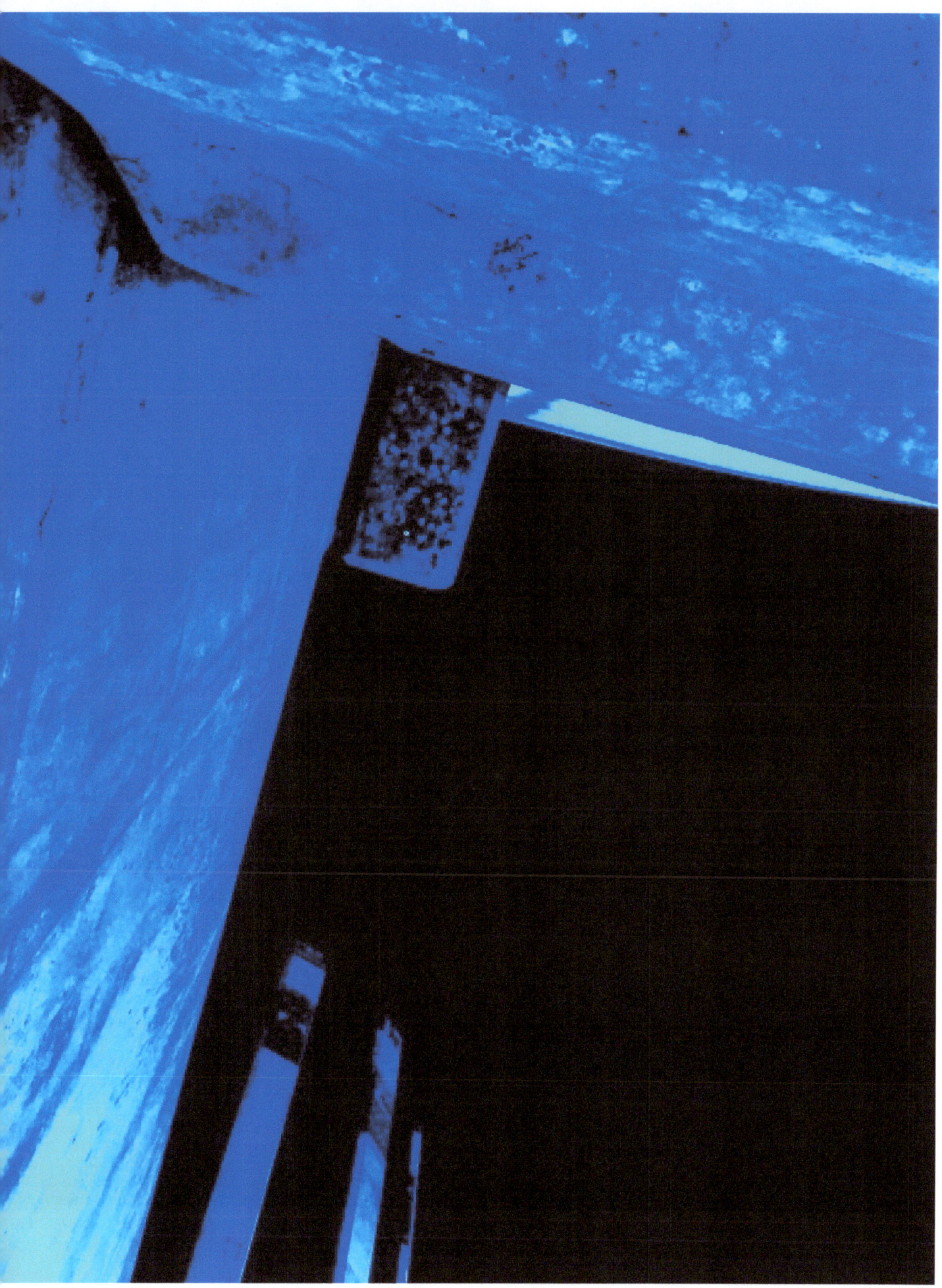

Blue Dam

July 2015

Boulder City, Nevada

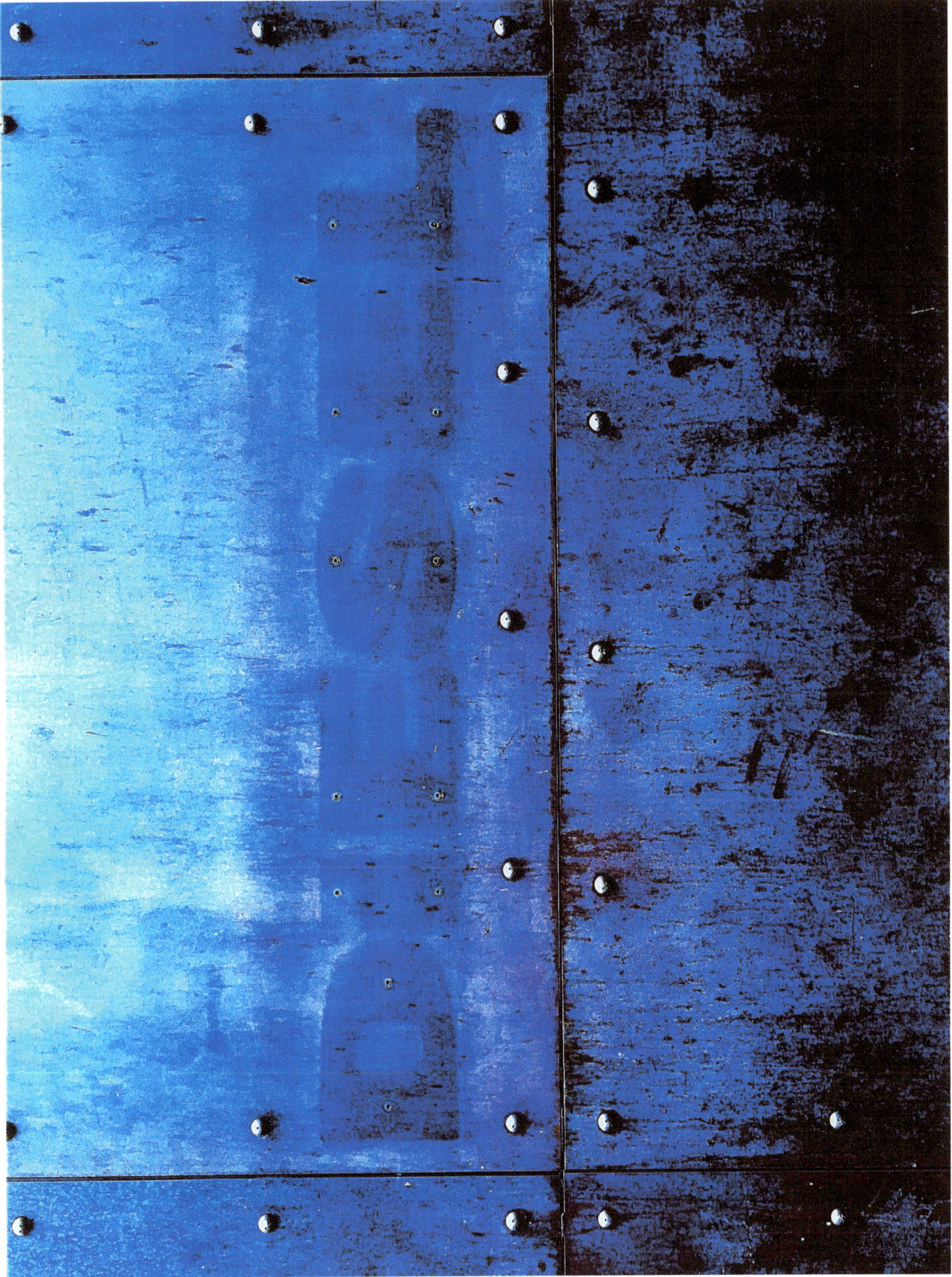

Blue Metal Facade II

March 2015

New York, New York

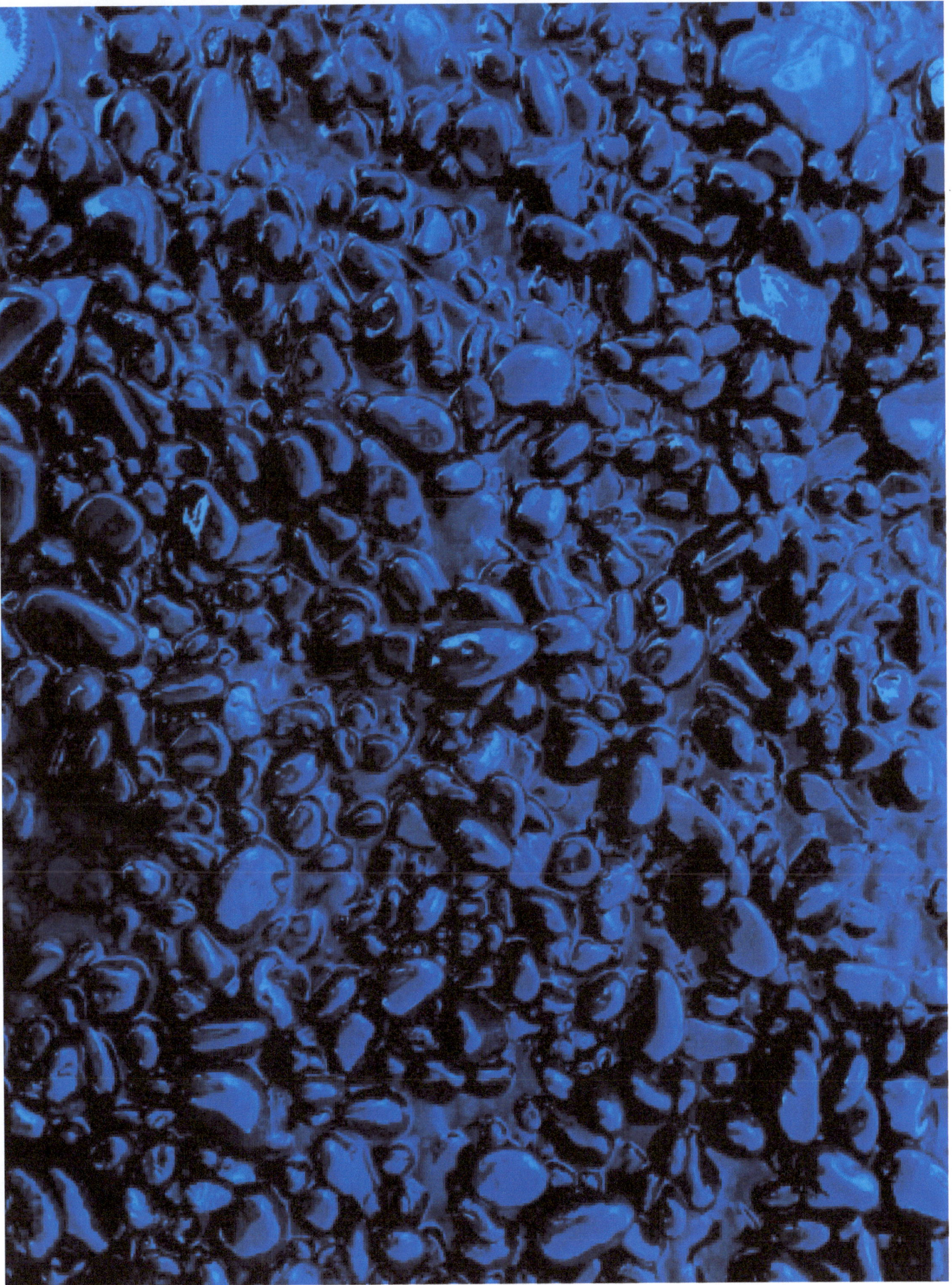

Blue Rock Beach

July 2014

Hana

Maui, Hawaii

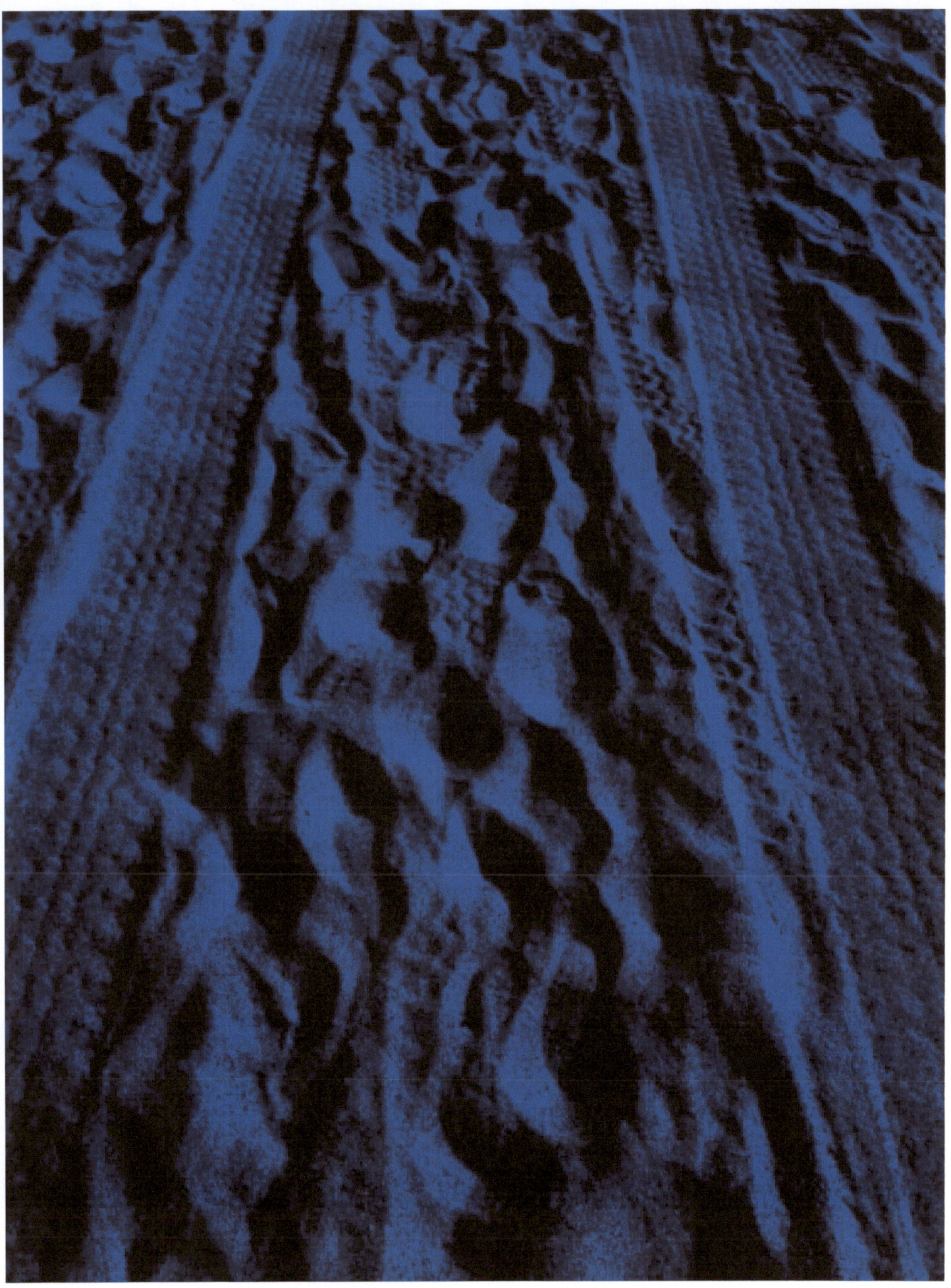

Tracks in Blue Sand

December 2011

Ft. Lauderdale, Florida

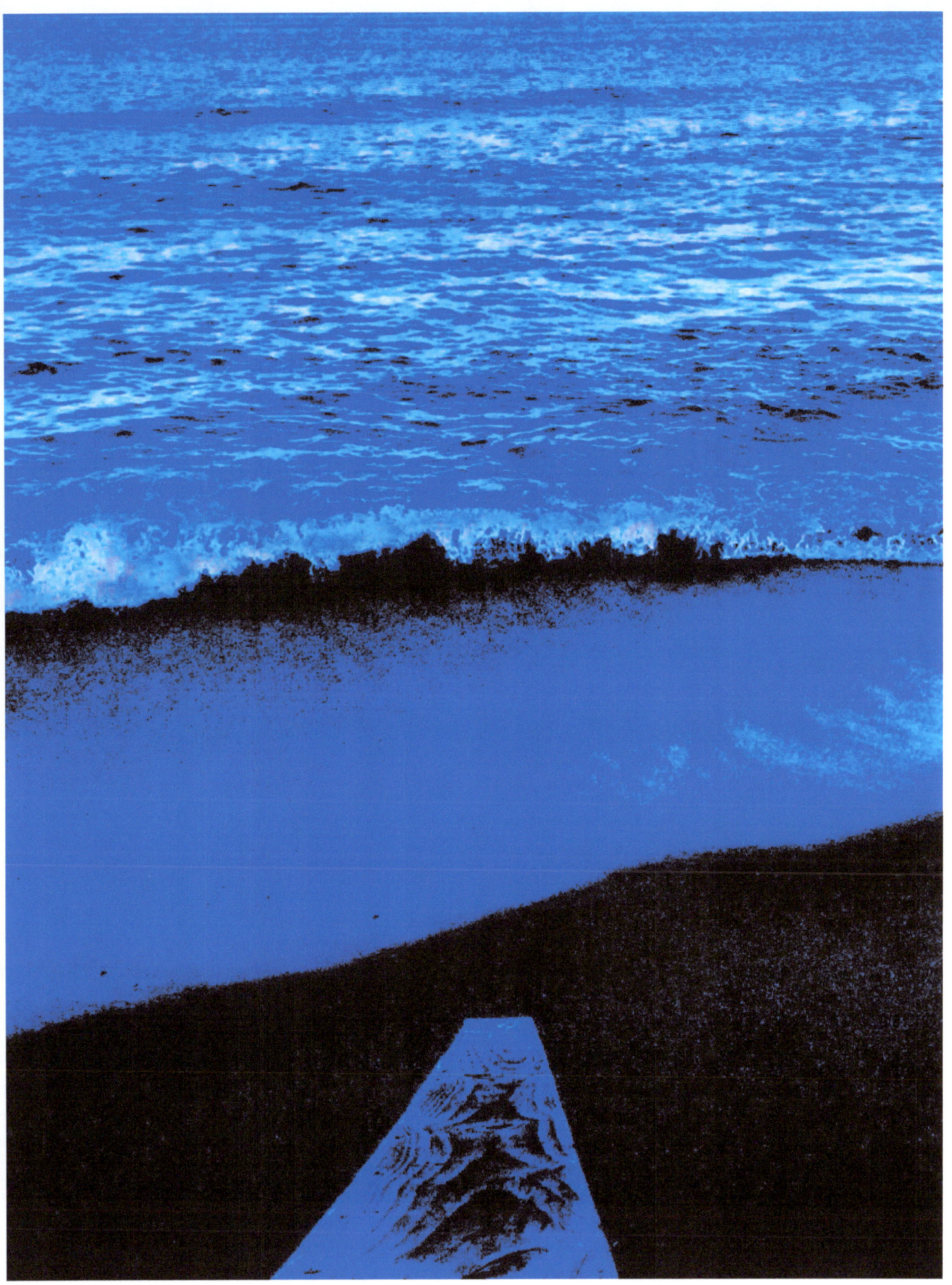

Blue Seashore

January 2015

Manalapan, Florida

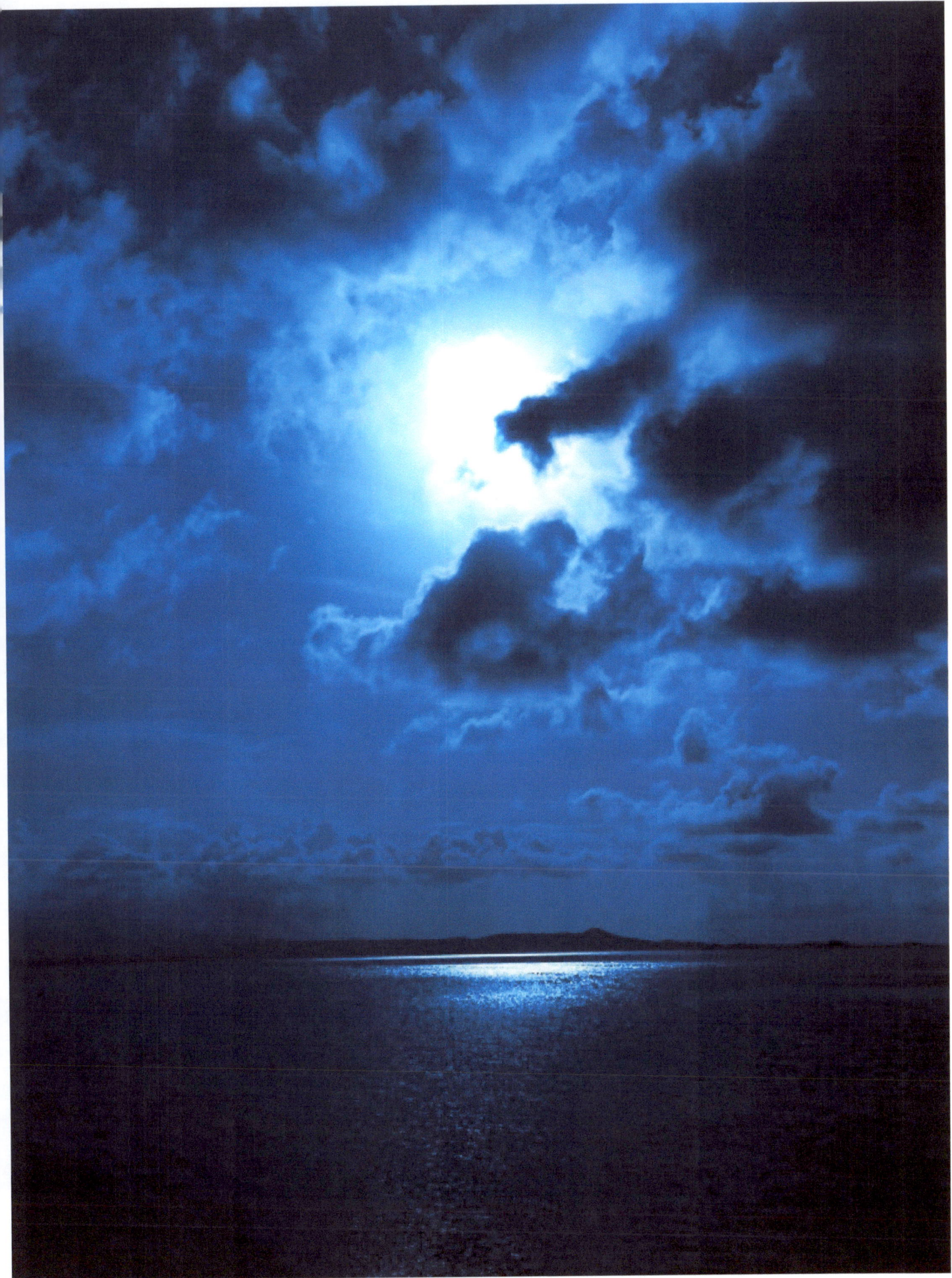

Blue Sky with Ocean

July 2015

Fajardo, Puerto Rico

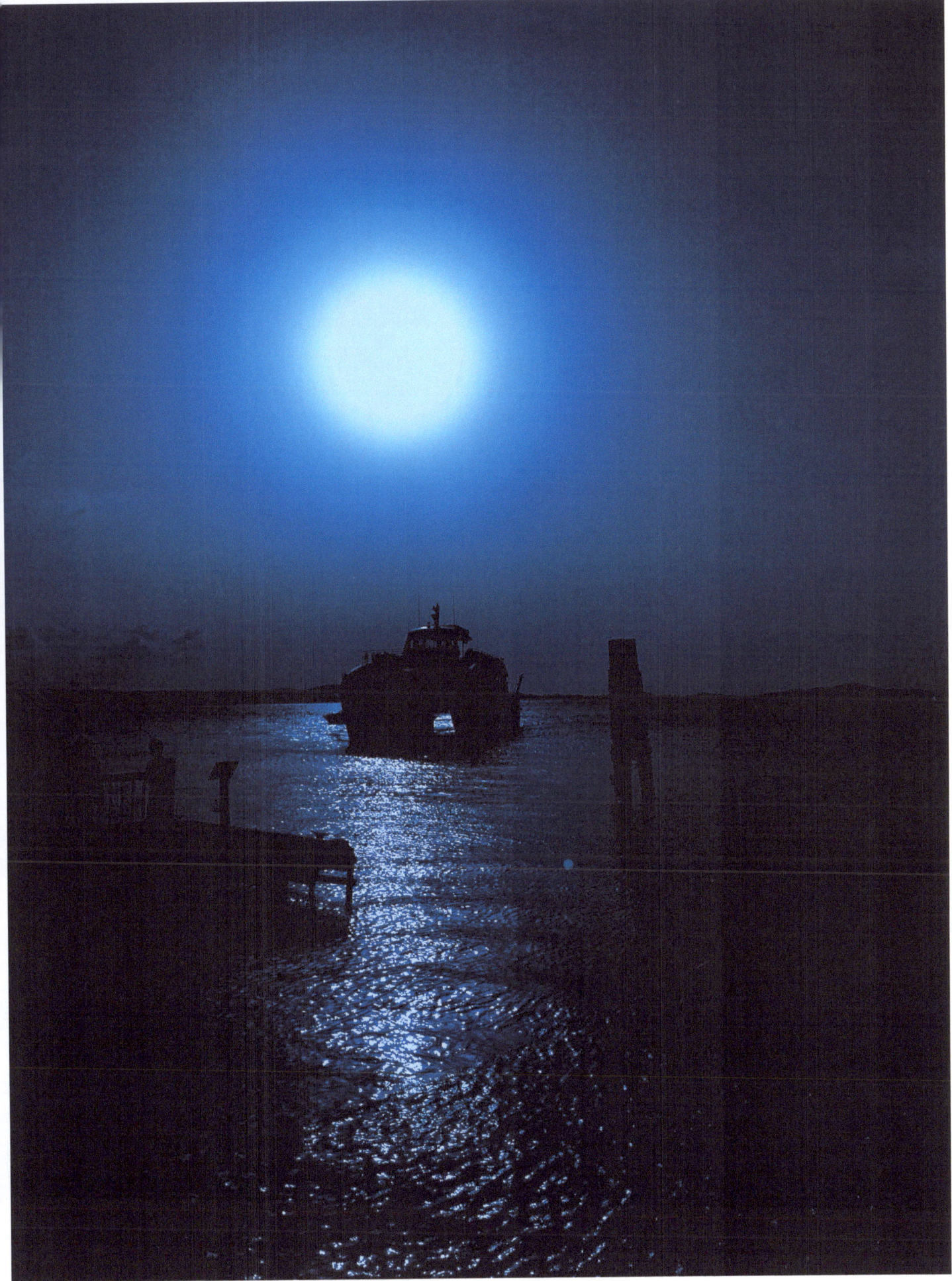

Blue Sunset with Boat

July 2015

Isla Palominos, Puerto Rico

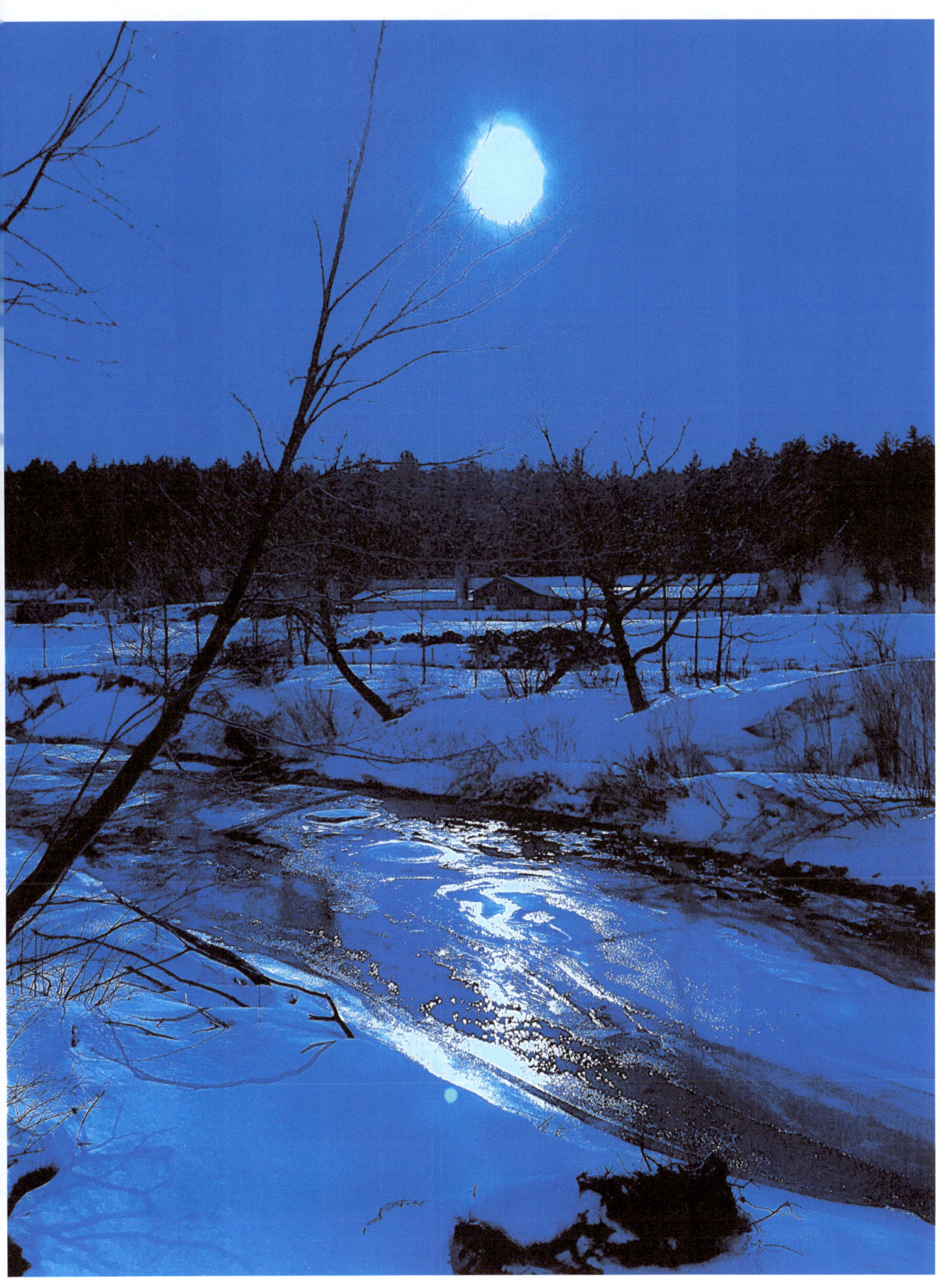

Icy Blue

March 2015

Stowe, Vermont

COPYRIGHT

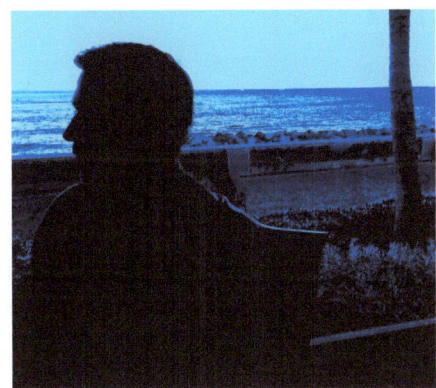 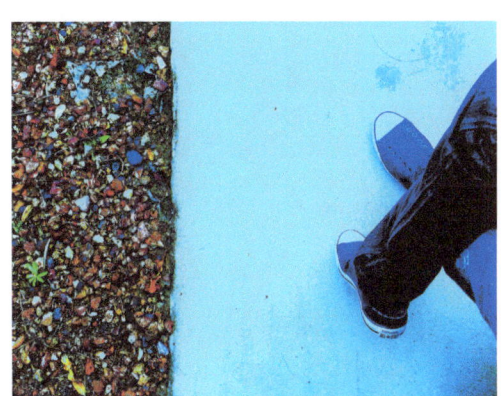